BOOKWORMS

Machines That Work

Big Diggers

Amy Hayes

Cavendish Square
New York

Published in 2016 by Cavendish Square Publishing, LLC
243 5th Avenue, Suite 136, New York, NY 10016

First Edition

Website: cavendishsq.com

CPSIA Compliance Information: Batch #WS15CSQ

Library of Congress Cataloging-in-Publication Data

Hayes, Amy, author.
Big diggers / Amy Hayes.
pages cm. — (Machines that work)
Includes index.
ISBN 978-1-50260-392-0 (hardcover) ISBN 978-1-50260-391-3 (paperback) ISBN 978-1-50260-393-7 (ebook)
1. Excavating machinery—Juvenile literature. 2. Earthmoving machinery—Juvenile literature. I. Title.

TA735.H39 2016
621.8'65—dc23

2014049166

Editorial Director: David McNamara
Copy Editor: Cynthia Roby
Art Director: Jeffrey Talbot
Designer: Stephanie Flecha
Senior Production Manager: Jennifer Ryder-Talbot
Production Editor: Renni Johnson

The photographs in this book are used by permission and through the courtesy of: narvikk/Getty Images, cover; TFoxFoto/Shutterstock.com, 5; Richard du Toit/Gallo Images/Getty Images, 7; NooScapes/Shutterstock.com, 9; SERGEY BOBOK / Stringer/AFP/Getty Images, 11; smereka/Shutterstock.com, 13; GIRODJL/Shutterstock.com, 15; Michael Jaeger, 17; bogdanhoda/Shutterstock.com, 19; © iStockphoto.com/jordan_rusev.

Printed in the United States of America

Contents

Diggers are big **machines**.

Diggers have a long arm called a **boom**.

At the end of the boom there is a big shovel called a **bucket**.

The bucket digs into the ground.

It makes a deep hole.

JCB

Buckets have teeth at the end of the shovel.

Teeth help break up the ground.

JCB
JCB

Diggers can do all sorts of things.

Diggers can dig holes.

Diggers can **dredge** rivers.

Diggers can break buildings **apart**.

Diggers are great workers!

New Words

apart (uh-PART) Into separate pieces.

boom (BOOM) The part of a digger that acts like an arm.

bucket (BUK-it) A shovel that helps a digger dig.

dredge (DREJ) To dig up to look for things or make rivers deeper.

machines (muh-SHEENS) Equipment with moving parts that are used to do jobs.

Index

About the Author

Amy Hayes lives in the beautiful city of Buffalo, New York. She has written several books for children, including the Machines That Work and the Our Holidays series for Cavendish Square.

About BOOKWORMS

Bookworms help independent readers gain reading confidence through high-frequency words, simple sentences, and strong picture/text support. Each book explores a concept that helps children relate what they read to the world in which they live.